Les Anomalies

PALMETTO
PUBLISHING
Charleston, SC
www.PalmettoPublishing.com

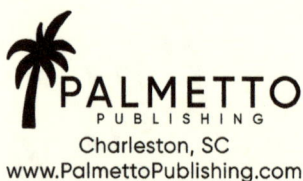

Paperback ISBN: 979-8-8229-2664-6

Les Anomalies

Maria El-Aswad

To all those who celebrated my anomalies and to all the fellow anomalies out there:
I celebrate you.

Table of Contents

Growing Pains   1

Beirut   19

I'm Alive   29

Anomalies   47

About the Author   66

Growing Pains

One

For in deception...there is truth.

In truth...there is change.

In change...there is freedom.

And in freedom, there is deception.

Two

I placed the hot straightening iron on the counter to cool off,

attached the last couple of bobby pins into her golden hair,

and ensured her jewelry suited the grand occasion;

with the final touches of mascara,

suffocating hugs, and proud gazes, we hurried out of that

hotel room.

We stepped off the train and headed straight for the reception,

where I saw my love finally put on the cap and gown.

She finally put them on.

Lost in the anticipation of capturing the moment, my heart

leapt with a frightful surprise as they called her name.

I childishly grinned while my palms reddened, then I cheered

as my mother—my idol—got her second PhD diploma.

Three

In difference, I felt similitude;
in similitude, I felt oddness.

My passive soul suffocated
while its pain couldn't scream.

It's torture, feeling wrongness
knowing righteousness,
while acting upon foolishness.

Who am I conforming to?
What if I don't want to conform?
Is that me conforming to nothing?
The "nothing" that is the something causing my imbalance?

I look at my own greatness from afar—
wishing, withering, wondering.

Have I shed enough blood over the plot?
Does it get better from here, or do I rot?

How lost have I been to have gone astray?
You can't capture me, even if you may.

In this chaos of mind,
through these bleeding tears,
would it be so unkind
to hug me out of my fears?

Who am I seeking?

The truth of survival
seems primal.

Love is the key—
I don't know if that's true still.
My light is no longer free;
this despair has left me ill.

Four

May I embellish the unveiling beauty?
May I hold her guilt?
May I riddle her certainty?
May she grace me with the portal tears have built?

May I interject
To offer a prospect
to a fear only her reconnaissance,
has put her through fence after fence.

Yes, I've had the audacious courage
to declare her achingly at a loss.
Be certain, to her battle—I pay homage
and to her solitude I embrace the cause.

Permit me to attempt;
to helplessly acquit.
Solely, she exempts.
The guised candor that I predict.

Engrain this direly,
for it might be a recurring epiphany.

Life is but a vision
of the choices we've conditioned.
Don't concede, for you will imprison
all her victorious intuition.

Five

Inhale the words, Exhale the Thoughts.

Grunts, Carvings, Paintings;
Symbols, Chants, Illustrations;
thoughts and words mating
while fountain pens are ruling nations.

Epiphanies transcribed—
discoveries italicized.

Outrageous accusations—
prolific alterations.

The reach of the mind;
its limits you will never find.
Webs of hard covers aligned
their authors remain blind.

The thrill of the chase—
to wander, to learn, to embrace.

The elitists, the Baggage'd Intellectuals—
they'll preach hubris about counterfactuals.

Don't scoff, just modestly overwhelm;
for with every edition, language steers the helm.

Six

I shall write this totem
mutually conceived as an emblem.
I shall encapsulate
apparent smiles of mine in retrograde.

Totem, I fear, is a lie misrepresented,
for I lack the constituents of verity
needed to graze a mind so conflicted
and thoughts to conceal the facades of transparency.

Fantasy opposes its submerged meaning,
its muses incandescently demeaning.
The attractiveness in its prelude—
the time of being—it protrudes deceiving the broken,
maliciously embracing the forsaken.

Amusingly thought to be liberating,
the cage of existing as freeing
powers of defeat hidden
behind the possibility of "God-ridden."

No slaughter of beliefs is afoot—
only the doubtful would have mistook.
Pose the question to the poser—
you'll know we're the loneliness connoisseur.

It is the blindness that corners;
it is the exasperating truth that bothers.
My aching reigns deep in continuum,
an existence so breathtakingly solemn.

Seven

A dash is what I'll draw
on the fractured cheekbone.
Let go; nothing wrong with being raw.
I won't cast no stone.

Join my scoff:
How could hollowness fulfill
and satiety restraints?
"Nothing" is the oxymoronic whip.
Thus, I declare:
Chronic perpetual loneliness
rests heavy on your temple's chain.

A civilized heathen, I'd prescribe
the condition of one passionate human.
I reckon the cycle is but a brainwashing bribe
to feed the debilitating end of your brethren.

It is indeed tragically appalling
that pitless depths only revive.
What superlative odds have I been navigating?
To balance what and not to archive?

You see, my fellow child:
Truths rank mild;
realities run wild;
thoughts reign beguiled.

Certainty amuses;
death—it chooses.
Love bruises;
trust—it ruins.

But, that's where we prosper—
Believers: true creatures of irony,
for destinies and journeys bicker;
the soothing illusion of predictions tire pitifully.

Eight

A game of catch;
a broken heart to patch.
Silence the reigning language;
a broken route to an obscene passage.

Finding habitual loneliness
while the pack is there to conceal.
A fluctuating set of sightlessness
and misery becomes the martyr's appeal.

Where does this thread thrive?
Rest your eyes and count from one to five.
A thin thread, it is so
separating the self-pitying from the foe.

She grins from reflection—
enlighten your solitude's perception.
She's no foe,
they've convinced you of so.

She feasts in fields of crimson tears
distorted visions of euphoric fears.
An iron fist on the mind of radiance—
no wonder she survives using conditional appearances.

Her wings aren't torn;
they do not need assertion—
they just haven't been born.
It shatters her to live by your validation;
to prosper and grow, crumble and fall,
before the warmth of her trusted hearts.

Requisites necessitate her dismal—
she'll kill herself before they part.

Her rigor for life branches
from the joys of their smiles it's watered.
She prays her soul gives her chances.
History repeats: the present is what mattered.

Contemplation, realization, perception—
they say don't give them attention.
She will not trade her "sinner's" mind for redemption.
She shall find, she hopefully believes,
the balance of my life's fruition.

Nine

Where's heaven?
Her obnoxiously tiny fingers tugged.

How long can you stay in heaven for?
Her concern grows.

But how can time not exist in heaven?
The eight-year-old shrieks.

Do you know someone who lives in heaven?
She innocently ponders.

Why are you crying, Mama?
Hugging her was a no-brainer.

What do you mean heaven's not in the sky?
She demands, feeling betrayed.

Mama, can I have chocolate milk if I eat all my fruits?
She sneakily requests.

Yes, I did finish all three cups of milk.
She lies.

Why do you have to go again?
She cries.

Are you going to stay far away like Baba?
She whispers.

How can forever exist if heaven has no time?
She welcomes.

How can I feel happy all the time if heaven doesn't
allow me to be present?
The ten-year-old perplexes.

Why did he tell me I'm asking so many questions?
She feels defeated.

No, Mama. I ate alone again and played in the garden.
She recites

If we don't die, then why do we live?
Still persistent at thirteen.

God is Love and Love is God—
she gets middle school praise.

Of course the devil's real!
She defends

Why can't I shut my door?
She snaps.

Practice went great!
The first of many covers.

I think I'm the best student in the class,
she winces and smirks.

Forgive me, father, for I have sinned—
the final straw.

Yes I'm okay, I just had a nightmare. I'll see you
tonight.
She drives off.

"Stop asking questions—just have faith and obey!"

"You're a sociopath. *No* one thinks like that"

"You're pathetic."

"Why do you think about these things? It's pointless, tiring, and annoying. Let me enjoy my burger.""

"I can't help you if you don't want to help yourself."

"Why is there always something wrong? Haven't we sacrificed enough?"

"You're ungrateful."

"Not everyone has the luxury to think like that."

"I think heaven is in the garden of Eden."

"What if heaven was on a comfy couch and had a large TV screen with a massive popcorn machine?"

"Spinoza would be so disappointed."

"Kant would be mortified."

"Camus would laugh."

Where's heaven? She asks.

"I don't think it matters," she smirks

"Cuz I think I might've embraced it a few times."

Beirut

Ten

August 4, 2020

At 6:07 p.m.   Gore.
       Gore portraits her wedding pictures.

At thirty-nine-years-old, Abdo Tanious Ata is confined by his own home.

At three-years-old, Alexandra Najjar is "safer" now.

At fifteen-years-old, Elias Khoury becomes the face of Our Pain,

          Our Anguish.

          Our Despair,

          Our Anger,

          Our Imminent Death.

At 1:31 p.m., 2021—*the* 200, known and unknown, remain decaying with the memory of the Cedar's Colors: fruition, music, creativity, celebration, family, health, and

       Hope

At 1:32 p.m., 2021—yet another tribute is written, for it is the only solace to misery that is offered.

At 1:33 p.m., leaders rest their heads on our backs and lay in their warm bassinets.

At 1:34 p.m., twelve-year-old men and women make supper, run through the bills, play music, and complain about homework.

Ten & One

I've lost track of their different tastes;
falling eight times did not help.

Who the hell knows?
They all taste damning—
Lead, Blood, Gore, Sweat and Garbage.

I miss the taste of the earth.
I miss kissing their bare feet.
I yearn to harbor the world's elite.
  Once more
they keep fleeing

Lift this corrupt concrete off me;
send these weighted tanks back.
    No—I mean, away...
        Back?
            Send these weighted tanks Back and Away.
I'm at a loss of words:
How many voyageurs overly enjoy their stay?

How many guests enslave their hosts?
    Destroy their homes?

Get these foreign poles out of me;
quiet these ungodly thunders.
Excuse me;

Apologies—
I meant: awaken my somber with your
"words of Justice, chants of Truth, and weapons
of Freedom."

    Seriously? Ammonium Nitrate?
    Do I dare ask why?

Enlighten me,
end my misery
Tell me.

Has my embrace suffocated you?
My shades enticed you?
My children outshone you?
My presence beseeched your rigorous aggression?

I am the child of my inhabitants;
I am the mother of their children.

Who would evolve off their mother's suffering?
        They've made me denounce my name.
    They've shamed my colors; their colors—my colors.

I shall keep holding on.
Barely: I am
holding on
to the hope of my children's growth.

I suppose a mother's faith is tested to deserve its testimony.

I refuse to fall a ninth time—
there are only so many times a phoenix can rise.

What was my name again?
I think the last one they gave me was *Beirut*.

Ten & Two

A message to all my fellow lost souls on their way to the
airports, hiding their runny noses behind their masks, and
sighing in defeat and contemplation.

Although I'm the last person to be an authority on good-
byes—a guru on managing our very complex essences,
thoughts, and emotions—I could not rest my eyes before
jotting this down.

I've learnt and am still contemplating three major "lessons."

1. Laughter is our tool.
    Laughter is our tool to make a mockery out of an unimag-
    inably cruel situation.
    You stand in front of your options and you can already
    feel the defeat emanating.
    We laugh, we laugh until we can't breathe anymore.
    We shriek and howl and gasp for air because we, at that
    moment in time, simply don't care.
    It's elegance at its finest: to smile and enjoy the fading
    hours, minutes, and seconds in the face of an ugly and
    very real truth.

2. Love is a growing constant. So generic, so cliche, and yes so cheesy, you might claim. But, here is where you forget that:

When you love how chocolate residue forms on the corners of their mouths—

When they are joyfully eating next to you—

When you love how they are wholeheartedly themselves and with you while you dance, implode, explode, and flourish with passion—

When you love to support and watch their broken back heal—

When you love to converse about nothing and giggle incessantly like children with no care in the world—

When you love unveiling the cold hearted mysteries of our mortal existence at 4 a.m.—

You gave your nonrefundable time and consenting effort, willingly, to a soul that just made you smile after reading this (and probably always will).

3. Belonging is our anchoring sanity.
We do not belong to a nation.
We, the voyagers, do not belong to a people—
we belong to our persons.

We are a mix of any walks

we have seen, lived, and been with a revolving door of cultures, peoples, propagandas and inclinations.
Our belonging goes to the souls that silhouette what we call home.

We are fluid and most of the time, wandering—but we have to have this certainty:

I will not fire the debate of belonging and survival. I'm not sure how one would frame survival right now. I just know that the people, the souls, the energies, and the voices of the people that we incandescently embrace are the balance to our sanity.
…That's all I have for now.

Maria El-Aswad

I'm Alive

Ten & Three

White knuckles, screeching soul;
gritting teeth, tears at war.

Raging gasps of air—
I refute the convergence of despair.
What can a crooked smile offer?   .
The services that seldom buffer.

Merely a tremble, a shake in posterior;
hours, gazes, reflections roar inferior.

What a bold dictatorship in disguise,
mere sustenance rendering one superficial prize.

Lips shut, turbulent eyes—
wishing, praying, pleading to rise.

Restoring the majesty of ink
a hand is reaching up high in the bottomless pit.
Intention's testimony is clear, despair's willingness to sink.
Flatter me; tell me: I shan't lose grit.

where agonies deafened
and hollow epiphanies threatened.

What tormented chambers are we?
To existence: I kneelingly plea.

Alter your essence and thrust me free.
Oh, what a fool was I
to deny that you coincide me;
from this horrid truth I shy.

The extent of your crippling loneliness resides,
its reflection on my mortality subsides.

Ten & Four

To accentuate your vigor;
to apprehend your rigor;
to alleviate your splendor—
mustn't I ferociously figure?

Turbulence seeps through structure.
What a manipulative ruse; organized chaos.
When I feel tenderness rupture
a submergent functioning, my biggest prowess.

The thought, a tumor,
defeat itself dethrones "prosper."
What a soothing lie put on repeat
to cry out and be the victim in obsolete.

The disillusion of time is paralyzing—
a gateway to slit wrists compensating.
I ponder the true nature of human;
a realization, a struggle, a fight, defeat—Satan?

Nowhere to run from your mind;
thoughts will forever suppress your bind
to the ultimatum of your kind.
How have I grown this consciously blind?

What was once known as an inevitable moment in time
is the continuum of your prime,
death mistaken for a single dime—
I have awoken to its malicious rhyme.

The want for the unknown's arrival
as the present awakenings cascade
to terminate what is known to me as survival.
Insanity: merely the knowledge of that dangling blade.

What should I recite
to the fugitive aliasing the prisoner's fight? What must I
do for this conquest?
Uncertainty? Or death at best?

How is hiding a feat rendered futile?
Don't they know they're their own exile?
Is that your answer to the vanishing grains?

Grinning teeth—
    what an absurd Reign.

Ten & Five

What could a gentle touch accomplish?
Mere palm's fragility
caressing more than a freckle or blemish—
a pounding heart is awakened suddenly.

What could unreasonable spontaneity offer,
other than a foggy mirror
Dilated pupils quivering with horror?
A soul's own reconnaissance—
here comes a tremor.

Arrows and a floating mind—
redemptions, reservations; one of a kind.
Universally but arbitrarily blind;
sweat and teardrops is what you'll find.

Where does a convicted fugitive rejoice?
Through misleading pleasantries?
For my deaf ears have graveled my voice.

Disowned by the grim clobbering back,
detached from the forthtold margins—
every unretrievable moment strategically set for an attack.
How to embrace my reality's weigh-ins?

Eagerly awaiting a moment's relief—
how can one abandon control's loss?
    Hysteria?
    Delusion?
        Human? Unprecedented grief.

Smile and dream: "who's boss?"

Refutation of my own victimization,
acceptance of my fearful damnation.
Freedom to the whitening discoloration;
joy to my broken restoration

I shall allow dissonance
    of the self that's exhilarated.
Certainty has baffled and decapitated
the very essence of generations emancipated.

Epiphanies are not awaited—
they are nothing short of fabricated.
Ruthless cries I celebrated—
cries that grew minds, liberated.

Ten & Six

Interlaced connections;
repetitive inquisitions;
pending collisions;
harboring emotions.

Stained sheets;
micro defeats;
nibbling doubts;
attuned laughs—no—scoffs.

To be youthfully driven
mistakenly at your prime.
Aging is forbidden.
Fine wine—that's the real dime

To be perceived as decadent
or, alas, Independent.
Foolish matters for the Hubris;
serene anguish for the fittest.

Ironic how they look to the other and misconceive.
Don't dare claim the only alternative to believe!

Uncertainty flatters the beguiled,
Certainty accentuates the mystics.
Perspective enchants the ponderers
Truth overthrows the metrics.

Fascinating, won't you agree?
Intuition has ascertained thee.
Unity of cosmic singularities
are freeing to the fluctuating propensities.

Either surrender to defeat—
defeat to surrender—
the flux manipulates currents;
nothing but to observe and absorb moments.

Ten & Seven

When It's Over—Purpose after COVID

No more looking in the mirror for too long
feeling defeated by flesh.
Its fragility: anomalous, annoying, atrophied.

Suffocating loops of hyperawareness: Why do we all kneel
before death's presence?
Teens, tweens, and millennials managing midlife crises.

Let's hope—no more of that.
More displays of eureka'd passions.
Tonight, expression finally overthrows faction;
more liberating existential fences;
more lending hands, underrated affection, overdue gratitude.
The Earth sends her regards.
Oh, by the way—

thought experiment with me.
What if: when it's over—if it's over—all that harms vanishes
with it?
Wave the magic science hypotheticals
You'll either meet a world of dysphoric extinctions or expand-
ing universals.
Ironic, isn't it?

Harm carries aliases?

When it's over—if it's over—
I will plead with the just Mother.
"Keep the beauty in all this pain;
birth us again,
decannulate our vain.
Keep the beauty in all this pain—
modest, grateful, present: I shall remain.
Not for a moment will they now dismiss Your Rain.
Keep the beauty in all this pain."

Ten & Eight

It's that exhilarating gasp
when laughter consumes
your presence in your grasp—
completely euphoric—now let's resume.

It's capsulating the overwhelming freeness,
lids so closely shut; tears escape.
Edge's relief…I transgress.
Oh, if only total surrender could be taped!

    They raise the dawning of death to a duel.
    Inexplicable outbursts of resilience;
    a tender shine warms the cruel.
    The blueprint to the reward of patience.

    Odd, is it not?
    When I wholeheartedly forgot
    the precedents of death and glory
    diverged to a point beyond me.

Aching tribulations have cost
to a timeless joy I offer:
    An intrigued mind encapsulated;
        a soul stumbling—surviving—
            further.

Ten & Nine

Permit me.
Bless me.
Enchant me.
Dumbfound me.

To zest for your stunning cacophony;
to rigor for your cunning scars;
to sway for your witty idiosyncrasies;
to grin for your sorrowful epiphanies.

Absorb your wrinkles' sparkle
Graze your skin's history.
Witness your mark's twinkle
Praise your wisdom's serenity.

Take your hand
Dance with the flux.
How insignificant the things we understand—
off you go—put on that tux.

Excuse my hidden messages
but proper attire is for the masses.

A tux of willingness;
a tie of tenderness;
a shirt of humility;
a jacket of dexterity.

Pants for the intrigued—
shoes for the persistent.
Cologne for the transparent—
cuffs for the uncharted.

The dance floor awaits.

Let's sway incessantly
Be ridden with melody.

My soul, it suffocates.
Heart beats off rhythm—
his presence infuriates.
Why endow him?

She; he; they—I interrogate.
Soar high Soar alone.
Branch your feathers, wait for fate—
blood for ice; heart for stone.

My soul, it suffocates.
My soul, it starves.
My soul, it yearns.
My soul, it overcomes.
My soul, it hardens.

My soul, it suffocates.
My soul, it crashes.
My soul, it yearns.
My soul, it heals.
My soul, it loves.
My soul, it feels.
My soul, it aches.

My soul, it lives.

It lives for tender au revoirs.
It lives for love powers.
It lives for fortified reunions.
It lives for joyful shrieks.
It lives for existing continuums.
It lives for earned peaks.

It lives for aching rain.
It lives for solemn nights.
It lives for wisdom pain.
It lives for passion flights.

My soul—

It sways; it loves; it lives.

Twenty

He is:

as good ice-cream is a remedy for sobbing;

as divine as the bed's embrace for the exploited back;

as tear-inducing as Bambi's mother;

as surreal as roller coaster heart drops;

as complex as human breath;

as loving as a newborn's gaze.

His paw in my palm—

his whiskers up my nose.

He purrs

while I grin for the finale.

Twenty & One

I didn't ask to exist.
I do exist to ask.

An agonizing loop—
let's just go to the rave.

Sway, shuffle, build the rhythm.
Cover your ears—trap the hymn.

I've spent whole circumferences
watching the handles slave.

Thinking as fear surfaces
Expected to adhere—no—"behave!"

My eyeballs sting
harsher than my mother's ring.

She said I crossed a line,
that I should've learned to harbor my mind.

Her beating heart and mine in dissonance—
I try to shield her innocence.

Appealing to a deterministic condemner—
    no, Savior—
let him save me from the pain he's instilled as a favor.

How am I to learn
    if I don't yearn?

For the mercy of the Trojan horse;
    to humble myself before his course.

Is it true that my anger gives them purpose?
    I should care less, I suppose.

My chest's weight latches
    to forcibly tearing being's sphere.

I did not ask to be here—
we're bread in batches.

I did not ask to be here—
I hate that I know this.
    Because
        I

            am

                Here.

Anomalies

Twenty & Two

Rest assured, I'm telling you—
malice is but a ruse,
a plot disguised, ingrained in supposed cues
Seemingly a heart to choose.

The fluctuation of retreat and defeat;
a pounding soul misleading a feat—
is it righteously so?
An embodiment of euphoria before the low.

When has an imprint of a smile healed
other than to a child refrained from need?

What is this madness of emptiness,
aliased with fullness, perpetuating helplessness?

Insanity is the admission of the fall,
Abolition the embrace of passion.
"Stand pious, strong, and tall!"
"Don't succumb to it; total demolition."

Ironic, pitiful are the cowardly shrine,
withstanding the miracle of neither a nickel nor a dime.
The blasphemy of the unilateral victim;
the rawness of effort and time.

Don't dare dismiss appreciation—
"love" is not merely a condemnation.

Its image toyed and punctured;
your soul, indubitably fractured.

Ruthlessly manipulated- crushed—
all to revive the innocence of rosy cheeks flushed.
The hollowness, the demise, the suicide—
no, you heart-wrenched broken pride.

The rise, the conquer, the win—
greater than denial is our "sin."

Time: what an asylum!
An unchosen ultimatum.
Who dares withstand an alternative?
The imbecile; the self-deceiving fugitive.

Here's the exposed secret:
Ironic, isn't it? In the cacophony of lonely.

Love: the four lettered maze.
An anomie to the citizens of "always."
Words: the translation of a timeless entity;
transcribing love beyond extremities.

A marvel in one's reality—
the only key to ensure their sanity.

An overture to the finale:
I beg to the cynics viewing this as a liability.

Loving isn't so subpar.
In fact,
I'd say:
love always.

Twenty & Three

Urges to express
sensibility, they digress.

Overwhelm me more, I plead!
Surrendering who I am to thee.

My beloved has taught me so—
a secret of the universe
that he himself doesn't know.

Every second I fall;
every minute I love;
every hour I enamor.

Loving you has given me a lesson about time.
Foolish are the physicists—
one needn't measure
what can only be treasured.

Every second I love begets every hour I am grateful.

Humbly, I am enlightened
with this very instance,
now one that's ridden.

will not be stamped on the timeline—
well, perhaps not one that isn't mine.

Feeling time, you baffle—

Time doesn't exist, Einstein recites.

Feeling time? You? Baffle.

Here she goes!

Time is merely a perception,
forcibly constant without exception.
That's the misconception.

Dare to rival the unanimity of the clock's hands;
let your mind create and cherish where it lands.

The secret that I speculate
is one of versatile bounds.
Time isn't inherently innate.

It is love's loyal companion—
once you sway with their irreplaceable idiosyncrasies;
once you synchronize with their breath;
once your soul creates because of their safety;

once your fingers interlace with theirs.

You will know that only then could you befriend time.

"Our time is limited," kindergarteners will chant.

Feeling time? You? Baffle!

A new nursery rhyme is afoot:

"One, two, three,
        tick tock, tick tock.
One, two, three,
        I love you and me."

Feeling time and measuring change. Standardizing growth,
I say to you:
Kneel.

For our time is as boundless as our love
should we choose to surrender while knowing that

those who don't know that gratitude supersedes time and
marries love,
are merely eighty years old.

Twenty & Four

"Enough."
A metric for completion—
it's no secret that I've never felt like I am enough.

Enough is a metric.
Odd, when we reaffirm our worth by a metric.
"You are enough just as you are."
As if worth can be quantified.

Could it be?
Let's play a game:
What amount dictates ample worth?
That's easy...
"Enough."

Let's rebel against the productivity trope
by reassuring each other that we can measure our worth.
So long as we realize that we needn't always produce;
so long as we realize that we are "enough."
"It, too, shall pass."

Someone please tell me:
How long will I need to swim in this bottomless pit that is
"enough?"
Oh wait—
I need to realize that I am whatever measure others allude to
my completion,
for how can a measure, measure anything if it not be comparative?

I'm enough—
I'm just enough;
I'm just enough for the collective.
I suffice.
I guess I'll always have to suffice.
To go by
under the illusion that I am anything greater than enough.

Twenty & Five

The word potential is misleading.

It's the Band-Aid made to cover unmet expectations;
it's the weapon used to force designated directions.

Potential is a funny thing—
it's what's said when you are not enough right now.
As if
right now isn't enough
because you see it isn't;
the future holds greatness of the unlocked potential.

We will never reach our "full" potential,
a mentality that's sickly praised.

Let's sell the illusion of a boundless bound,
run, run, run, till you get tired and realize that you could've
skipped, walked, or perched on many other grounds.

Potential is a limiting thing—
it's limited by measurable success.
Sure, let's teach the six-year-old that she has potential;
that one day,
if she works hard enough,
she will be lucky to have that potential recognized.

Careful now—
not too much recognition.
The future holds the greatness of unlocked potential.
Her worth just is her measurable success.
How else do we keep whole nations in check?

Sure,
stick her in all kinds of classes to develop her "potential."
Watch her never enjoy anything again in her life.
She'll be thirty years old, learning to have fun again and love
deeply,
with her overly attached cat at her side.

"You've got great potential kid. You're beaming with it. You will
make a great impact in this world, I'm sure of it."
How can dialogue be simultaneously uplifting and soul crushing?

I was told, I am told, and I will probably still be told, that I
have great potential.

But to my darling daughters, sons, and everything in between:
"You're here, look at you! I can't imagine anything better than
this moment; to be in the presence of your greatness."

Twenty & Six

It's audacious and cruel,
thought to be meticulous and prude—
the condition of being in a world of demarcated seeing.

Will you be my candor? I plead.
To my finger stains I impede
the inhabited mirror that concedes
with whichever turn it is pleased.

At a poser's quarrel
you have found my impasse—
grim, intoxicating positivity does excel
only in between four walls and an "alas."

Wings set you behind bars.
Why would you soar?
When you could walk and end up to par.
Imprisoned minds; your feathers they tore.

Embroider it on
the aura of selfish survival.
Believe me—it weighs a ton
until you mold into their "optimal."

Only then will you graze
the bloody stitches stained.
Their wrinkled lids will wave you praise;
their scars will ensure yours don't remain.

I shall not need to pinch you—
I salute your daring fight.
It needn't be facetious nor true,
that now you see there is no black and white.

Yet again we welcome a new voyageur.
My sympathies to your new collisions.
I'm afraid you're no stranger
with a mind full of contradicting inquisitions.

Twenty & Seven

It's comical how

rocks turn into silky pillows
when dawn and dusk look the same;

moldy meals turn into a queen's feast
as soon as one starts counting them.

Tea time? Coffee time?
Let's just sit down.

They told me they've had the worst possible week—
a sentiment they shared a week prior.

They told me they were at their threshold;
a truth they've confided the last three years.

They told me they feel unseen,
that the desecrated deemed them a means to an end.

They told me they've lost their zest,
that painting in the park is all they needed.

They told me insurance keeps denying
the antidepressants, catalyzing their cycle.

They told me that waving at a dog
was their only joy nowadays.

They told me they're exhausted;
blamed themselves for being another victim.

They still believe the world is good,
even though they could never deserve such a thing.

That'll be $20.14—together or separate?
I took care of the check.

They looked at me teary eyed
and sang their chorus of the week:

"You made my day. How did I ever get so lucky? One
day I'll be able to afford this."

They gave me an impactful embrace.
I went to work,
clocked in,
put my apron on and thought:
Who knew God preferred tea over coffee?

Twenty & Eight

She seduced the light first.
She simply was—
and then there was thirst.

She lay on unformed rivers,
waiting to be called upon—
her cue was the shivers.

Brilliance she inspired;
innovation she motivated;
mystery, she desired.
Herself—she hated.

The poet's fountain pen;
the sculptor's fable;
the slave's legend;
the ruler's table.

She took—

vibrant as the petals may be;
elusive as meaning ought to be—

she claimed.

As feet twirled in square sequences;
as blood meshed with teras;
as the cortex braved consequences;
as the neonate touched fear.

She oversaw—

as pilgrims chanted and cried;
as "outcasts" spoke sinister;
as witches were "tried;"
as nations bowed to a minister.

She sustained—

She was feared;
she was revered.
Hated, she felt.
Fetishized, she knelt.

She's been confused,
She's been loved.
She's been dismissed,
She's been praised.

I've read;
I've seen;
I've witnessed;
I've felt.

Whole tongues, mystics, and enthusiasts
obsess—

unlimited power;
inadvertent reign;
unbinding freedom.

No one seems to see the shackles.
They rot, she rusts.

And yet—

even time's a genius.
Life's pen

does not recognize.

She's at the center of it all.
A captive—
> hated,
> adored,
> feared,
> misunderstood,
> bound,
> lonely,
> essential.

A captive we've all come to know as: *Death*.

About the Author

Maria El-Aswad has a Bachelor of Arts in Psychology and Philosophy. She has been writing poetry for 10 years now. This is Maria's first published poetry book. Her aim is to help societies' deemed 'anomalies' feel heard, seen, and included. Maria was raised in Lebanon and her writing includes homage pieces to her home and the injustices it faces. Maria was encouraged by her entourage to publish her writings and she finally did. She explores the limits of tradition, culture and precedents. 'Why?' is her favorite question. More than anything Maria has remained authentic to her creative self through her writing and hopes to connect with her audience through it.

9 798822 926646